Wedding
Speeches
and Toasts

Other titles in:- 'The Wedding Collection'

The Complete Wedding Organiser & Record
The Complete Wedding Video Organiser
The Best Man's Organiser
Your Guide to Planning The Wedding Day
Getting It Right: Wedding Speeches
Getting It Right: Your Wedding Planner
Getting It Right: The Best Best Man
Getting It Right: Wedding Etiquette

Wedding Speeches and Toasts

by Barbara Jeffery

foulsham

LONDON • NEW YORK • TORONTO • SYDNEY

foulsham

Bennetts Close, Cippenham, Berks, SL1 5AP

Edited by Carole Chapman

ISBN 0-572-00779-5
Copyright © 1991 & 1993 W. Foulsham & Co. Ltd.

Photoset by Typesetting Solutions, Slough, Great Britain.
Printed in Great Britain by
St. Edmunsbury Press, Bury St. Edmunds, Suffolk.

Contents

Introduction

'They're getting married!' . . . 'We've named the day!' . . . statements to bring immediate warmth to the heart.

So, why are you reading these words? The chances are that you've been quickly shaken from your 'happy pedestal' by the directive that followed the statement — 'Of course, you'll have to make a speech!' — and that you are looking for the answer to your weak cry of 'Help!'

The prospect is probably a daunting one but it need not be so – with the knowledge of a few elementary rules, good advice, some preparation and a little practice there is absolutely no reason why anyone cannot do it. Let's face it, very few people can rise and deliver a speech off-the-cuff without any preparation. It should be encouraging to know that it is not difficult to make a wedding speech, they are relatively short and by the time you're ready to start, the audience will be warmed by the happiness of the occasion and do not expect or want lengthy slick professional performances.

This book is for those who are faced with such a duty. You could be the bride's father, a relative of the bride, the bridegroom, the best man or the best woman! or even the bride!

If the wedding is close at hand, dip into this book and digest as much as you can. At the very least, your self-confidence should be boosted. You'll even find ready-made speeches for a range of situations that you can adapt as your own.

However, if the big day is well into the future, read on without too much delay. Apply yourself, and you too will join the ranks of highly competent wedding speech-makers of whom they say, 'Didn't he/she speak well!'

CHAPTER ONE

Speechmaking — Who says What and When

We assume, in this book, a traditional English wedding. However, the ideas and guidance given will be useful if you have to make a speech at any wedding.

If you are in any doubt at all as to which type of wedding is being planned, you are strongly advised to discuss what will be required of you before you start preparing your speech.

Different cultures and different faiths have their own traditions. For example, at Jewish weddings, often the groom speaks after the best man and the final toast may be to Her Majesty, the Queen. Scotland has its own customary order of speeches, but this is not always followed strictly. Irish weddings may be different again;

unpredictable both for the number of speakers and for how long they go on. Caribbean-style weddings tend to be exuberant festivals of colourful clothing and ethnic music, sometimes with little regard to the time of day or ideas of being there on time. Asian weddings usually follow a clearly-defined pattern particular to each faith, where everybody knows how things are done. Inter-faith marriages are on the increase, and may involve two weddings, so the parties have to make their own rules about speeches.

The traditional English wedding reception may be formal, semi-formal, or relaxed, with many guests or with just a few. It may be held in a hall or a restaurant or at home. The speeches made at such receptions are expected to be quite short — each lasting for, at most, four or five minutes — and they involve either proposing a toast or replying to a toast. Usually, they are made after the wedding breakfast — whether a set meal or a buffet — has been taken, and before the wedding cake is cut. Incidentally, when a toast is proposed, all who are able, stand and raise their glasses to the person or persons being toasted, who remain seated.

At larger receptions the speechmakers may be introduced by a professional toastmaster. Generally however, brief introductions are made by the best man.

The order of speeches and what is said, is quite logical. The opening speech is made by the bride's father; he is followed by the bridegroom; finally the best man speaks.

To start off the proceedings, the toastmaster (or the best man) asks for silence and introduces the first speaker.

Bride's father

If the bride's father is absent for any reason, the speech could be made by whoever has given her away, or by a mature male family relative or friend. The specific content obviously depends on the relationship of the speaker to the bride, but assuming that it is her father who speaks he will speak on behalf of his wife and himself and may express:

- a welcome to the groom's parents, relatives of both families and other guests;

- how proud they are of their daughter;

- a story about the events leading up to the wedding;

- a story about the bride's earlier life;

- congratulations to the groom;

- happiness in getting to know the groom and his family;

- confidence in the couple's future together;

- a few words of wisdom to the couple for the start of their future life together;

- that they are sure that all guests would want to join them in wishing the couple well;

- the toast to 'The Health and Happiness of the Bride and Groom'.

Bridegroom

The groom speaks on behalf of his wife and himself. His speech is mainly to thank people who have been involved in setting up the wedding. He may express:

- thanks to the bride's father for the toast;
- thanks to the bride's father for his daughter's hand;
- thanks for the wedding and reception;
- thanks for the words of welcome into the family;
- his own happiness and how fortunate he is to have such a lovely bride;
- praise for the bride's parents on having brought up their daughter so well;
- his luck in joining his wife's family;
- thanks to his own parents for his upbringing;
- a response to any advice given by the bride's father;
- an amusing story about how he met his bride or any problems which have been overcome;
- thanks to the guests for attending, their good wishes and generous gifts;
- thanks to the best man, ushers and any helpers;
- admiration for the beauty of the bridesmaids and gratitude for their participation;
- his wish to present the attendants with gifts;
- the toast to 'The Bridesmaids'.

Best Man

The best man responds on behalf of the bridesmaids. As most of the necessary thanks have been given, he has the opportunity to entertain the guests with witty comments and funny stories. He may express:

- the bridesmaids' thanks for the toast and for the gifts;
- a few of his own compliments to the bridesmaids;
- admiration for the bride and the groom's luck in having such a lovely bride;
- congratulations to the bride and groom;
- pleasure in carrying out his duties;
- a toast to 'The Bride and Groom's Future Happiness';
- his and the guests' thanks to the host and hostess;
- a toast to 'The Host and Hostess';
- a toast to 'Absent Friends';
- the sentiments and senders of any messages and telemessages;
- the programme for the rest of the reception.

This traditional order and content of speeches is fine in an ideal world. But, we wonder, how many weddings are there that take place within an 'ideal, happy families' environment? What if this is a second marriage? Perhaps the bride's father is dead — or her parents divorced? Perhaps the groom's parents have divorced and re-married? Are both families happy about the marriage?

Have the bride and groom been living together for some time before deciding to wed? Has either of them been coping as a single parent? These are all possibles in the real world so, before you write your speech, do make tactful enquiries and seek advice from those arranging the wedding. In this book we shall cover some of the non-ideal possibilities, but we cannot allow for them all.

Then again, there is change — progress, if you like. In today's world: the bride often wishes to make a speech or say a few words; a distinguished guest may be invited to speak at some length; there may be no bridesmaids; there may be a best girl instead of a best man, or even two best men; the bride and groom may well take over the arrangements and the cost of the reception themselves, thereby being the hosts. So, do enquire before you write your speech, and save yourself, and others, embarrassment on the day.

CHAPTER TWO

Specimen Speeches
(Conventional Situations)

Having acquired as much information as you can about the wedding and all who are involved, you are ready to prepare your speech. By far the simplest way to do this is to select a specimen speech from this chapter or from Chapter Three — the speech that seems most suitable for the occasion — and change the names and facts appropriately.

Even if you prefer to write your own speech, it's probably worth your while to look briefly at some of the specimen speeches, just to get the 'feel' of them, before going on to Chapter Four.

Toast to the Bride and Bridegroom
(proposed by the Bride's father)

Specimen 1

'Ladies and Gentlemen — I'm afraid I am not much of an orator. In fact, I think the last speech I made in public was at my own wedding. Now, how long ago was that? One grows so forgetful as one grows older.

'We are so pleased to welcome you all here today and we feel sure that none of us will ever forget what a perfect picture Jean and Stephen made as they stood together in church. Mind you, Jean was so late starting out that I began to wonder if you'd all have turned up for nothing. But she made it in the end. Ah, well, it is the bride's privilege. She told me the reason she was so late was that she couldn't get her veil right.

'You all saw that she got it right in the end — and everything else as well. I dare say Stephen didn't mind waiting for a girl who finally arrived looking such a picture.

'In any case, I am sure they have such a long and happy future stretching before them that a few minutes here or there makes little difference. It doesn't matter so much, after all, if you are married at two o'clock or ten past two — so long as you are married to the right partner. And I have never been so sure of anything in my life as that these two have done just that — found the right partner.

'People always say at weddings something like, "I hope their married life will be as happy as my own". I'll add to that. I'll say I hope their married life will be as happy as my wife has made my own. For it's a good wife that makes a good marriage — and that's just what Stephen has managed to find.

'So, Ladies and Gentlemen — Friends — I ask you to rise and lift your glasses, as we drink a toast of long life and great happiness to the bride and groom. (Pause) To Jean and Stephen!'

Specimen 2

'Ladies and Gentlemen — Will you please stand, and raise your glasses, and drink with me a toast to the health, happiness, and prosperity of the newlyweds. (Pause) To Paula and Simon!

'Today is Paula and Simon's celebration. It's the big day they have been waiting for. And, they have dropped a very broad hint that I should keep my speech short so the guests can enjoy the day with them. I'm sure they didn't mean it quite like that — at least, I'm almost sure !

'Well, to all of our guests we say, "Thank you so much for being here." Mary and I are delighted to share this day with so many dear friends and relations from both families. Particularly, I must mention Simon's parents, May and Arthur; two grandmothers and two grandfathers; two great-grandmothers; and both sets of godparents. And, I must not forget those who have travelled a very long way to be here.

'For those of you who don't know Paula very well, I can tell you that she is a daughter to be proud of. Yes, I know fathers are biased! She does have a mind of her own, as I dare say Simon has discovered. It's said that, when the bride walks up the *aisle* to the *altar* and sings a *hymn*, she is saying to herself, "I'll . . . alter . . . him!', I'm told they all do it, Simon. They all do it!

'As for Simon — well, Mary and I and all the family hope very much that he doesn't get 'altered'. During the months we have known him, he has shown himself to be kind, caring and reliable. In fact, exactly the person we've

17

always hoped for as a son-in-law. We don't feel we are losing Paula; we feel we are entrusting her to Simon's good care.

'Most of you know that, after the honeymoon — and I'm threatened with the family rolling-pin if I even hint where they are going! — Paula and Simon will be moving to northern climes to set up their first home. So, I'm sure you'll agree that I could do no better than give them — from all of us — the Old Gaelic Blessing: (Read, if not memorised)

"May the road rise to meet you,
May the wind be always at your back,
May the sun shine warm upon your face,
The rains fall soft upon your fields,
And until we meet again, may God hold you
In the palm of his hand."

(Pause) 'Ladies and Gentlemen — dear Friends — Thank you!'

The Bridegroom's Reply
(and Toast to the Bridesmaids
or Matron of Honour)

Specimen 1

'Ladies and Gentlemen — Jean and I want to thank you, George, for those kind words and good wishes. Needless to say, we are both delighted to be here today!

18

'Sarah — I must now think of her as mother-in-law — has worked so hard making all the arrangements for our big day. And George — father-in-law! — has, so he tells us, considered taking out a second mortgage as Sarah got on with the planning. Jean and I are so grateful to them, not only for this wonderful reception, but for letting us share their home until we can set up our own. Our sincerest thanks!

'And I must thank my own parents for all they have done for me over the past twenty-mumble years. They have been marvellous. . . . No, Mum made me promise that I wouldn't tell you my age. She said it would make her seem old! . . . Looking at her today, you'll all agree she could have been scarcely three years old when she had me!

'I'm sure you'll all agree that I am the luckiest man in the world. I have wonderful parents and parents-in-law. I have a beautiful, intelligent and hard-working wife. Actually, she has a long list of qualities — but I can't decipher her handwriting . . . ! And I have such marvellous friends and relations, here to share the day with us. My wife and I want to thank you all for coming to our wedding, and for your very generous presents. Thank you!

'We are both particularly pleased to see Jean's cousin, Polly, who flew in from Vancouver only yesterday, and Uncle Fred, who made the long journey down from Newcastle especially to be with us. And, I'm sure, we are all thinking with affection of those who aren't able to be here today.

'I see, out of the corner of my eye, that Peter, my best man, is getting impatient, waiting to make his speech. So far, he's been a perfect best man, I'm sure you'll all agree. I say 'so far' because we haven't heard his speech yet!

'You see, he did tell me a rather ominous best man story. *This* best man was asked to include in his speech verse 18, Chapter 4, of the First Epistle of John, which reads: "There is no fear in love; but perfect love casteth out fear." Unfortunately, he read, instead, from the Gospel according to St. John, and came up with, "For thou hast had five husbands; and he whom thou now hast is not thy husband." After that story, I thought it safer to leave the content of Peter's speech entirely up to him!

'However, he does have the duty of replying to my toast to the matron of honour. Jenny has been absolutely marvellous. Not only has she looked wonderful, but she has given wonderful support to Jean, both today and throughout all the preparations.

'So, Ladies and Gentlemen — please stand and lift your glasses and join me in this toast to the matron of honour. (Pause) To Jenny!'

Specimen 2

'Ladies and Gentlemen, and especially Paula's parents and my own Mum and Dad!

'Will you all please rise, now, and raise your glasses with me and toast our lovely bridesmaids, Diana and Lucy, and our handsome page, Dean. They have contributed so much to this, the happiest day of our lives, that my first words of thanks must go to them. (Pause) To the bridesmaids and the page!

'What has really made this the happiest day of *my* life is the lovely girl sitting next to me. Public speaking is not my scene, nor can I easily find the words to say how wonderful Paula is. In fact, if it wasn't for getting married I wouldn't even be here! I really am a man of few words, and never more so than now.

'But on behalf of Paula, and myself, and everyone else here, I do wish to say "Thank you", a really big thank you, for the splendid reception given to us all by Paula's parents, and for this marvellous feast. Their helpfulness and generosity is very evident both here at this reception and in the help they have already given to Paula and me in setting up home.

'I'm impressed by the number of people who have rallied round in all sorts of ways. If you're not mentioned by name, that's most of you, please be assured that Paula and I are very grateful.

'For my parents too, this is a great day, in which they also have played their part. They looked after me in sickness and in health, as I well remember! They supported and encouraged me through the years up to now, so, to the best Mum and Dad in the world, what more can I say than those simple words, "Thank you very much indeed"?

'Paula and I also want to say "Hello" and greet those relatives and friends who have travelled miles to be here today, from so many different places.

'And special thanks to Terry, for being best man. Though I'm not too sure, yet, just how thankful to be, since we have still to hear his speech!

'Then, to make sure we include everyone, Paula and I want to thank you all for your good wishes and generosity. As soon as we can, we will write to thank you, personally, for your thoughtful gifts.

'Finally, I want to say that there is one gift that has come to me personally and to me alone. This is a gift you cannot buy. A gift without price, yet a real treasure; I speak of the young lady sitting next to me! So, it is with real appreciation that I say to Mary and Bill, for the gift of a lifetime: "Thank you, both of you, for Paula's hand in marriage." '

The Best Man's Reply
(on behalf of the Bridesmaids or Matron of Honour)

Specimen 1

'Ladies and Gentlemen — One of the traditional rewards of a best man, is being allowed to kiss the matron of honour. However, I've kissed Jenny many times. So I asked Stephen if, instead, I could spend the weekend with her. Stephen said, provided she hadn't made other plans, he thought it was definitely "On".

'I think I'd better explain, for those of you who don't know us well, that Jenny and I were married just over a year ago! Stephen was *my* best man and Jean was chief bridesmaid. Need I say more? . . . Except, perhaps, *theirs* must have been *quite* a kiss! Look where it's got them today!

'So, it is with extra-special pleasure that I thank the bridegroom for his kind words and toast to the matron of honour, and for his gift — a really lovely brooch — to her. And, of course, I thank him for asking me to be his best man.

'Stephen particularly requested me to tell one of my jokes, today. I went through my bumper book of clean best man's jokes — I think that should be my bumper book of best man's clean jokes. I spent a whole week learning the one about the wrong chapter of "John" and the five husbands, so I could tell it to you with all the actions! And what does Stephen do! — He steals my joke! Watch out Jean! Be warned exactly what kind of a man you have married! A clean joke stealer!

'So, all I have left is my quotation. No best man should be without a good quotation in reserve. Mine is actually a very serious line, from Tennyson: "A happy bridesmaid makes a happy bride". You only have to look at Jean, to see that is certainly true of her.

'Now, I have to thank our hosts, on behalf of everyone here, for such a marvellous reception. And to wish the bride and groom all the very best in their life together. Many of you have asked me how old Jean and Stephen are. There's a simple answer. Old Jean and old Stephen are doing really well! Long may it continue.'

Specimen 2

'Ladies, Gentlemen, Friends — Is there anyone here who is neither a lady, a gentleman or a friend? . . . Right, then, — and Others. I do have to make sure I include everybody!

'All weddings are excuses for celebration. That's the first reason for me being here! The second reason is that I didn't have to pay to come in!

'Seriously though, this is the wedding of my very good friend Simon to a very lively and lovely lady, Paula. And, they asked *me* to be best man! That's something very special. I thank them for that privilege. I did wonder if they might have wanted somebody rich and famous! But, they decided to settle for me. Poor and infamous!

'My first task is to reply to the groom's toast to the bridesmaids and the page. On their behalf, I say thank you to Simon for his kind words and for his gifts.

'Next, I'd like to give the newlyweds the traditional best man's wish. For good luck, good health and happiness, and may all their troubles be little ones! I'm sure you'll all agree that Paula and Simon are a marvellous, well-suited couple, and they thoroughly deserve all the happiness they're going to share together.

'Many weddings have a touch of fairytale romance about them. This one certainly has! Paula brings the romance into it, while the fairytale is that Simon is *my* friend. The truth is that I'm *his* friend — and I ought to know better.

'Paula and Simon remind me of the story about the princess and the frog. Unfortunately, though, no matter how many times she kisses him, he doesn't turn into a prince. Never mind Paula. Keep trying! Now you know why Simon and I get on so well. It's because he is such a tolerant chap. He's also much more modest than I am — but then, he's got a lot more to be modest about!

'Finally, a piece of advice for Simon. When you move into your new home, and there is talk of DIY, always put off until tomorrow what you are going to make a mess of today. Then, you and Paula will have the happy life we all wish for you.

'And for you, Paula, remember the young bride who put up a notice in her kitchen saying "SMILE!" Nothing happened. Then, she changed it to one that said "SMILE ANYWAY!" And it worked!

'Our warmest wishes go with you, Paula and Simon. Fare ye well!'

* * *

At the end of the best man's speech, it is usual for him to read out the names of those who have sent congratulatory telemessages, giving the actual greetings (after 'editing' any that are of a too risqué nature!) from several of these. The remainder are left displayed for the guests to see, later.

If the bride wishes to speak, the best man should introduce her, briefly, if there is no toastmaster at the reception.

Following her speech (or immediately after the tele-messages if she is not speaking) the best man should advise the guests what is happening next in the programme. He may also be asked to tell them the plans for the remainder of the celebrations.

The Bride's Speech

There is no need for the bride to say anything at all at the wedding reception. In fact, traditional wedding etiquette provides no place for a speech from her.

However, bride's speeches are becoming more popular. What began as the bride's friends insisting on an impromptu speech, is nowadays anticipated with some speech preparation by the bride — just in case. Or, the bride may particularly wish to say a few words.

The ideal place for the bride's speech would be immediately after her husband has replied to the toast to the two of them. But, following on immediately from the toast to the bridesmaids, her speech, especially if she proposes a toast, will be 'out of place'. It is more appropriate then, for the bride's speech to be the last one, just after the best man's reply.

Generally, the bride's speech is short — a few sentences, from the heart, will be more than adequate.

Specimen 1

'Ladies and Gentlemen, our families, and all of my friends — It is very kind of you to insist that I break with tradition and speak to you all. I'm very pleased to have the opportunity, actually, of joining my thanks to those of my husband, for your help, support and your wonderful gifts to us.

'I'm not going to say very much, except that life is full of surprises and that Stephen is the best surprise that's ever happened for me.

'To see so many friends here, along with the best Mums and Dads in the world, our wonderful Godparents and all of our relatives, makes our day absolutely perfect. Thank you all very much indeed.'

Specimen 2

'Friends, family, all of you — Everyone has said, "Don't make a speech, Paula, you'll only weep all over the wedding cake!" I probably will, but they will be tears of happiness, and Simon has a large hankie ready. See what a considerate husband I have!

'I just wanted to say thank you, myself, to my parents for their patience with me and their understanding, over the years. But especially, thanks for this wonderful reception.

'And, I wanted to thank you all for sharing our day with us. It may be a while before we all meet up again, so I'd like to propose an extra toast, if I may. No, there's no need for you to stand or raise your glasses; because *this* is *my* toast to *you*. (Pause) To my wonderful husband; To our loving families and friends: I drink to your good health and happiness, always.' (Bride, alone drinks the toast.)

CHAPTER THREE

Specimen Speeches
(Unconventional Situations)

Toasts to the Bride and Bridegroom
(first marriage for both)

Bride's father deceased

When the bride's mother is a widow, the toast to the bride and groom should be made by a relative of mature years (an uncle, for example) or an old family friend.

Specimen 1

'Ladies and Gentlemen — Cheryl's mother, Sheila, has done me the great honour of asking me to propose a toast to the bride and groom.

'When I asked why I was chosen, Sheila said, "Well, you have known Cheryl since she was in rompers!" Which, I suppose is as good a reason as any. I should perhaps add that David was well into 'flares' when I first met him!

'Both Sheila and Cheryl have asked me to mention Cheryl's father, Tom. Of course I will. Tom was a wonderful friend, husband and father. For sure, he's looking down on us today, so proud of his little girl. And also, for sure, he wouldn't want any of us to be sad on such a day. He would have told a good joke. So, here's one for him. A young maiden and a handsome farmhand were walking home along a country road one evening. The lad was carrying a chicken in one hand, a cane in the other, and leading a goat. On his back was strapped a large bucket. When they came to a dark lane, the maiden said, "I'm not going down there with you — you might try to kiss me." "How on earth could I do that?" asked the lad, "when I'm carrying all this." "Well," said the girl. "You could stick the cane in the ground, tie the goat to it, and put the chicken under the bucket!"

'Yes, you've guessed right! Both Cheryl and David are in farm management! They met at college. What David did with the chicken, I don't know, but it wasn't long before they announced their engagement. They are lovely people. They have a bright future in store. I know you will all want to join me in wishing them every happiness in their life together. So, please stand and raise your glasses to the health, happiness and prosperity of Cheryl and David. (Pause) To Cheryl and David!'

* * *

When the father of the bride is very recently deceased, the bride's mother may decide that there should be a short tribute to him before the main speeches. Such a tribute would be appropriate should any close relative die just prior to the wedding. It is best made by a friend of the family and of the deceased.

Specimen 2

'Ladies and Gentlemen — John's family have asked me to say a few words at this point, and I'm glad to do so. Everyone knows that John was so looking forward to this day. Sadly, this was not to be. Perhaps we can remember him in two ways. First by a quiet moment and then by going ahead with the reception, just as he would have wished. (Pause, head bowed, for about 15 seconds.)

'This world is a better place for John having been with us. Our lives are richer for knowing him. (Pause) And, now, Ladies and Gentlemen, let us go ahead with Sally and Mark's big day.'

* * *

Alternatively, the relative or friend proposing the toast to the bride and groom, may be asked to pay tribute to the bride's late father, in his speech.

Specimen 3

'Ladies and Gentlemen — It is an honour and a great pleasure to be here to help Virginia — or Gina, as most of us know her — and Tony to celebrate their marriage.

'As many of you know, Gina's late father, Eric, was my kid brother. Many was the happy hour we spent, kicking a football around, or sparring at the gym, when we were younger. I remember I was with Eric when Gina brought Tony home to meet the family. We all got on so well. I know Eric was so looking forward to the wedding.

'We, today, are fulfilling his wishes for Gina and Tony. He is with us in our hearts and in our memories.

'Tony has been a marvellous friend to the family, always ready to help and give his advice. I know how highly Gina's mother, Sybil, thinks of him. And so do we all.

'As for Gina, well, how very beautiful she looks! The family is proud of her. We all believe that she and her husband have a wonderful life ahead of them. Do remember though, Gina, the words of A. P. Herbert: "The critical period in matrimony is breakfast time!" Over the years, I have spent several breakfast times with Gina. Let's be generous and say that she is one of those people who takes a while to wake up properly in the mornings!

'Virginia — Gina — and Tony, all of us here want to wish you a long, happy, healthy and prosperous future together.

'So, Ladies and Gentlemen, will you please stand and join me in this toast. (Pause) To Gina and Tony!'

Bride and Bridegroom already living together

This situation is becoming increasingly common in modern times. The bride's father may well wish to face the facts and show his complete acceptance of them, by the way his speech is worded.

Specimen 4

'Ladies and Gentlemen — Today is Carol and Philip's big day. The world belongs to them, and we are here to join in the celebrations.

'As most of you will know well, Carol and Philip are very independent young people. They even insisted on making all the wedding arrangements themselves, and, what's more, on footing the bill! Wasn't that marvellous of them?

'When, two years ago, the pair of them decided they would become life partners, we of the older generation — Marjorie and I, and Philip's parents, Sylvia and Jim — were just a bit concerned. *Would* it last, we wondered. But our fears were unfounded. I, certainly, don't know of a happier couple.

'Since then, their careers have gone from strength to strength. And every spare moment has gone into making their new flat a real home. Obviously, they're good for each other.

'A few months ago, Philip called in one evening. He said he'd left Carol fixing up shelves because he had something important to ask me. It turned out that he'd come round to formally ask for Carol's hand in marriage. Nothing could have pleased me more. When I told Marjorie — and when she had stopped weeping with joy — she said, "Do you know, they're already the most married couple I've ever seen."

'Today, knowing each others strengths and weaknesses

well, they signed the marriage contract. My job as father of the bride, is to propose a toast to them. This I do with great pride. Ladies and Gentlemen, will you please raise your glasses to Carol and Philip to join me in wishing them long life and good health, success in all they do, and may the happiness they have shared be continued for ever after. (Pause) To Carol and Philip.'

Bride is a single parent

When the bride has a child by a previous relationship, most guests at the wedding will be aware of the situation, but some may not. It is as well to mention the child in the speech made by the bride's father, but in a positive way. This — if nothing else — prevents the raising of curious eyebrows when a small boy or girl clasps the bride and calls her 'Mummy'!

Specimen 5

'Ladies and Gentlemen — There is nothing in the world that could have given more pleasure to my wife, Margaret, and to me, than seeing our youngest daughter, Belinda, looking so radiantly happy. We welcome you all here to share this special day with us.

'We know Belinda's husband, Tim, to be a kind, generous and understanding person — and not bad-looking either — so Margaret keeps telling me! As most of you know, that beautiful small girl who has been crawling around the floor, singing happily to herself for the past five minutes, is Belinda's daughter, Alison. Tim loves his new daughter very dearly. He told me, just now, that he almost wept at his own wedding when Alison called out, in church, "What's Mummy and Daddy doing now?" We are proud to have him as our son-in-law.

'Tim's parents, Sue and Charlie, are pretty wonderful people, too. Today, they've become instant grandparents and they tell us they are really thrilled at the idea.

'It's now my pleasure to propose the toast to the bride and groom. I hope you'll all agree that I should be a little unconventional, though, and include young Alison in the toast, because she is very much a part of this marriage.

'Ladies and Gentlemen, I ask you, please, to stand and raise your glasses to the long life and continued happiness of the newlyweds and their young daughter. (Pause) To Belinda and Tim — and to Alison. May God bless their lives together.'

Bride's mother or a female friend makes the toast

There is no reason, except tradition, why the person proposing the toast to the bride and bridegroom has to be male. There are situations where the bride's mother is the obvious choice as speechmaker. Perhaps the bride's parents are divorced and her father — for whatever reason — is not at the wedding. The bride's mother could have recently remarried and, by making the speech herself, she could avoid the father or stepfather problem. Or, the bride and groom could simply request that she makes the speech — rather than a male relative.

Again, in this modern age, the bride may ask a close

friend — perhaps her chief bridesmaid — to make the toast. Provided that all involved are happy with this and don't feel neglected or rejected, a close female friend makes a good choice as proposer of the toast.

Specimen 6

'Ladies and Gentlement, dear friends — Welcome to all of you. How pleased we are to see you all here, joining us in celebrating the marriage of Miranda and Duncan.

'As most of you will know, Miranda is my dear daughter and, because we have always been so close, she and Duncan begged ne to make the opening speech. I was, and am, absolutely thrilled at the idea.

'Miranda and I have been on our own since she was a very small girl. I am sure she will agree, we have had a good life together, not only as mother and daughter, but also as best chums. I even knew that Duncan was the right man for her before she knew it herself, and I really am happy to find that, today, I not only have a super daughter — but I've got a super son-in-law too.

'And, I've acquired a whole new family! Duncan's parents, Marie and Bill, have adopted me into their lives; I have much to thank them for — not least for all their willing help in making this day such a success. Thank you both!

'Now, I'm supposed to offer the bride and groom advice and words of wisdom. I had looked out a suitable quotation but, as we left the Registrar's this afternoon, the sun suddenly broke through and lit up the happy faces of my daughter and her husband. And, the thought that came to my mind at that moment has replaced the quotation as my wish for them both.

'Dear Miranda, dear Duncan, whether the clouds threaten or the sun shines, hold on to your love and be as happy, always, as you are today.

'Ladies and Gentlemen, please rise and join me in the toast to the bride and groom. (Pause) To Miranda and Duncan.'

Specimen 7

'Friends — It will probably seem strange to you that a chief bridesmaid is making the speech proposing the toast to the bride and groom. Jacqui particularly wanted me to do this because, of all her friends, I've known her the longest and best, and because — as she is always reminding me — I never stop talking, so I might as well use this to good effect!

'Jacqui and I met in our prams about twenty-four years ago. We played together as toddlers and were always in the same class at school. She was always a beautiful girl, kind, friendly and rarely flustered. I was a tomboy and usually rushing around in one panic situation or another. Yet we were inseparable.

'That is, until Bill came on the scene. Then it became, Bill this, and Bill that, and Bill's going to become this, that, and the other. I was quite sure it wouldn't last — especially when this handsome young man went off to college — and I stood by, in true pal's fashion, to pick up the inevitable pieces when all the "Billing and Cooing" came to a halt.

'But, as you all know, it didn't halt at all. Jacqui and I went to work for the "Listening Bank"; Bill finished college and went stock-broking in the city; and all was letters, whispered phone calls, and rushing up to town for concerts, film and cuddles in the park.

'. . . And that was *my* life! . . . What Jacqui and Bill got up to, I've never found out but, just a year ago, they announced their engagement. Most of us here today went to their celebration party, and it was there — so I've been told — that I promised to be chief bridesmaid and to make this speech. It must have been quite a party!

'As usual, I've been chatting on and on, but I do want to be absolutely serious for a moment. In all sincerity, Jacqui and Bill, I wish you all the good luck and happiness in the world. And I'm sure that, you, their friends, will echo that wish by joining me in the toast to the newlyweds.

'Will you all please stand and raise your glasses. (Pause) To Jacqui and Bill — Good luck and happiness, always.'

Toast to the Bride and Bridegroom, and the Bridegroom's Reply (second marriage for either, or both)

When the bride, or groom, or both, are marrying for the second time, being widowed or divorced, the toast to the

couple is normally made by a male friend, ideally the best man if there is one. It is not good form to refer to earlier marriages in detail. The speech is usually quite short.

Specimen 1

'Ladies and Gentlemen — It is a great pleasure for me to propose the health of Sandra and Ray. All marriages are special. Second marriages are doubly so. They are a time for renewed hope.

'I think all of us here today were really delighted when Sandra and Ray named the day. We'd all realised a long time ago that they were *so* well-suited. We began to think that they'd never realise it themselves.

'Ray, you said to me earlier today that you both knew how fortunate you are to have found another *chance* of happiness. We believe you will *find* that happiness. We wish you all that life can offer and hope that "the best is yet to come".

'Let us raise our glasses, then, to the bride and groom and to their happy future together. Ladies and Gentlemen (Pause) To Sandra and Ray.'

* * *

The reply by the bridegroom is, normally, the only other speech made at a second wedding, and again, may be quite short.

Specimen 2

'Ladies and Gentlemen, Friends — My wife and I are so pleased to see you all here, sharing our day with us. We thank you for your good wishes and for your under-standing. And we are very grateful for your kind and generous gifts.

'Sandra and I were a bit overcome when my dear daughter and son-in-law, Elizabeth and Philip, insisted that we hold our wedding reception in their lovely home. We thank you both for the loving thought. And Sandra insists that I thank you both, publicly, for taking *her* young daughter, Karen, to your hearts. It is wonderful that we are, already, such a close and happy family.

'Long may we continue so. And may all of you here today, meet with us on many future happy occasions. Thank you!'

Toast to the Bride and Bridegroom (at a very small and informal reception)

When there is only a handful of guests at an informal reception — perhaps in a small restaurant or a pub, a very brief toast may be considered more appropriate. This can be made by the bride's father, the best man, or anyone who knows the couple well. The bridegroom's reply may be just a few words of thanks.

Specimen 1

'I would like to propose a toast to Julie and Paul, to wish them every happiness in their life together. May all your troubles be little ones! (Pause) To Julie and Paul.'

*   *   *

41

Speech from a Distinguished Guest

At some larger weddings, a distinguished guest who knows the bride and/or the bridegroom well, may be invited to speak at some length. He or she might be someone respected in, say, the business or academic world, or perhaps a member of the clergy, or a sports or entertainment 'personality'.

In such cases, the distinguished guest's speech is normally the only speech, as such, made. With the conventional three or four speeches, followed by a long speech, the reception would be more like a seminar!

Instead, the conventional speeches are replaced by just a few words and the appropriate toast or reply. For example, the bride's father might say, merely: 'Reverend Smith, Ladies and Gentlemen — I would like to welcome you all here today, to celebrate the marriage of Felicity and Gerald. Will you please rise and lift your glasses and join me in this toast to the health and happiness of our young couple. (Pause) To Felicity and Gerald.'

At the end of the best man's brief reply for the bridesmaids, he should introduce the distinguished guest. He, or the bridegroom, should say a few words of thanks at the end of the speech.

Not all people who might be regarded as distinguished guests are experienced in public speaking. Those who are, may well have never been asked to make a wedding speech before. The following specimen speech is for them, and may also provide ideas for others, preparing their own, shorter speeches.

Specimen 1

'Ladies and Gentlemen — It is always a pleasure for me to attend a wedding, especially when I know the bride and groom so well. Today, I feel particularly honoured, since I have been asked to speak as a distinguished guest.

'Somewhere in this speech I'm supposed to say words of wisdom to the happy couple. And it did occur to me that, like most people who fill in forms or sign contracts, Michael and Angela may not have read the small print of the marriage contract. I see some heads nodding in agreement.

'Of course the problem is that there's so little written at all, let alone in small print. There's no party of the first part, as in the famous Marx Brothers' sketch, and certainly no sanity clause, as when Chico says "You gotta be kidding boss. There ain't no Sanity Clause!"

'Some people would say there ought to be a sanity clause in the marriage contract! Or at least a Government health warning! Maybe a FIMBRA-type notice saying shares can go down as well as up!

'With that in mind, I set out to survey the words of the wedding service to see just what people let themselves in for. I'm using the 1662 version of Cranmer's Prayer Book, for those who still care about such things, rather than the more recent computerised version, known as Series 3.

'For example, the Banns. Pretty well gone now. These

were designed, originally, to deter dowry hunters, carpet-baggers and small-time Jack-the-lads. They told seventeenth century swingers that you don't have to put a rope round your neck in order to ring the bell a few times!

'Marriage is not to be taken lightly or wantonly. Lovely old word, "wantonly". Reminds me of the schoolboys asking a spinster schoolteacher, "Please Miss, what's a harlot?" "A harlot is er- er- a wanton woman." "Right Miss! We all know what she's wanton!".

'We're told that marriage is ordained for procreation, but to prevent fornication! A subtle difference. Followed by words about those not having the gift of continency getting married. Strange doctrine! Sounds like: don't get married unless you have to.

'Wilt thou have this woman . . . ? "Wilt" is what some blokes do! Or, as at the proverbial Murphy's wedding, when the priest says, "Wilt thou have this woman?" and Murphy says, "I will if nobody else will!".

'Now, all this stuff about "forsaking all others" is often misunderstood. King David and King Solomon "didn't", as the old verse tells us:

"King David and King Solomon led merry, merry lives,
With many, many lady friends, and many, many wives.
But when old age came over them, with many, many qualms,
King Solomon wrote the Proverbs, and King David wrote the Psalms!"

44

'That reminds me of the two boys at confirmation class, trying to sort out the difference between polygamy and monogamy. "It's easy," says one. "When a man has more than one wife, that's polygamy. When he has only one wife, that's monotony!"

'If ever there was an urgent need under the Trade Descriptions Act, at least for a Government health warning, the marriage vows should be the prime candidate. I imagine today's happy couple didn't read the small print when they signed the register. No doubt they were so over the moon that they didn't read between the lines. I know none of us have, but that's no excuse! So following the old adage that the grass is always greener on the other side of the fence because that's where you've just come from, let's have a rather light-hearted look at what we let ourselves in for when we jumped over that moon and into the unknown.

'To start with, the vows are first spoken by the poor chap himself, the groom. Is his mind clearly on the job, as you might say, when he says: "I (and says his name) take thee, (and says the bride's name) for my wedded wife . . ."? How on earth does he *know* what it *means* to have a wife? Perhaps all bridegrooms should read Francis Bacon. He said, amongst numerous other things: "Wives are young men's mistresses; companions for middle age; and old men's nurses."

'If the groom's mind isn't on the job, the bride's certainly is. It's an old joke, but a good one with some truth in it, that when the bride goes up the *aisle* to the *altar* and sings a *hymn*, what she really means when she says her vows is, *I'LL ALTER HIM!*

45

'*To have and to hold.* All that means is, they have and they will.

'*From this day forward* . . . Misleading. The groom thinks it means the wedding day. Whereas the bride has already decided this when she first spotted the groom in the pub with his friends.

'*For better for worse, for richer for poorer.* This sounds heroic. It has also been misheard as an invitation to polygamy, allowing either spouse up to sixteen partners, as in *FOUR* better, *FOUR* worse . . . !

'*In sickness and in health.* Well, it's a good idea to make sure you've both got a BUPA card!

'*To love and to cherish, till death us do part, according to God's holy ordinance.* That's fine if it just refers to the pair of us. But do I have to take on board your ravenous family and their dreadful feuds?

'*Obedience* is rarely mentioned these days. No wonder — the woman used to promise to obey, but didn't. The man didn't but did!

'*And thereto I plight thee my troth.* By the time you reach these words or their modern equivalent, it's too late. By my troth, what a "plight" thou art in now!

Of course, the real crunch comes with the final pledge made by the groom alone. *"With this Ring I thee wed"* . . . That's all right I suppose, except that the word ring has a capital "R", which really means with all my capital, real, borrowed or mortgaged, I thee wed!

46

'With my body I thee worship. This isn't as obvious as the adolescent humorists think. It means, to get married, a man's body needs a thick skin, a broad back and a malleable posterior!

'And finally, *With all my worldly goods I thee endow.* These medieval words need updating, but surprise, surprise, they haven't been updated. That's because they appear to mean "What's mine is yours"! And here, as so often, there's a hidden meaning. The hidden meaning is that what's mine is yours, but just you try getting your hands on it! More to the point, only the groom spoke these words! That's because the law of the land at that time, 1662, assumed that the woman not only had no property, she *was* property. Which of course is why the bride's father "gives her away" — to the groom.

'So, it's not surprising that, *With all my worldly goods I thee endow* is missing from most modern wedding vows. Besides, in novels from Jane Austen to the Victorians such as Trollope and Dickens, women of marriageable age appear, all helping their mothers in the hunt for husbands. It still goes on! Weddings are great occasions for meeting your destiny! They're also occasions for meeting your past. Take a good look around now! "In the war of the sexes, nothing perplexes like meeting your exes!"

'But I digress. Another reason why most modern marriages omit the words about "All my worldly goods", is that the Married Woman's Property Act over a hundred years ago, permitted women to own and retain property of their own after marriage. So the words "worldly goods" had come to mean, "what's yours is mine, so I'm merely giving you the title to what was yours originally, before your father gave it to you"!

'The old system had led to some hilarious consequences. For example, some fifty years before the 1662 prayer book, Shakespeare, after writing all those romantic love sonnets — some of them addressed to blokes, it seems — wrote a will leaving his wife his second best bed!

'But "worldly goods", now, means everything from a Porsche, a villa in Spain, a houseboat, a Canary Wharf flat, right down to the Marks and Spencer Y-fronts, I suppose. Everything that isn't actually mortgaged, sold and leased back, or made the subject of a court order! "Flexible friends" and numbered Swiss bank accounts are excused!

'Still, you can't beat the old advice that matrimony means that penny buns cost twopence; three pence eventually; fifty pence at Sainsbury's; and five quid at Harrods.

'And yet. And yet. The wiser of the old generation will tell you that you can't keep accounts in families. And long before Shakespeare and Robert Burns sang their songs about the love of men and women, the Jewish Talmud, the collected wisdom of the rabbis, was saying things such as "A man should spend less than his means on food and drink for himself; up to his means on clothes for himself; and above his means on honouring his wife and children". That's what "With all my worldly goods I thee endow" means. In practical terms, Angela, you're advised to live within your means. If you can't live within your means, live within his!

'Now that we're all perfectly clear about the meaning and importance of reading the small print of contracts, I must give Angela and Michael SOME credit for their better judgements concerning some of the large print, that's to say I'm glad, and I'm sure you'll all agree, that from the list of hymns for the service they chose to ignore my selection for some of my old favourites, which included: Fight the Good Fight with All Thy Might, God Moves in a Mysterious Way. It Fell Upon a Summer Day and Suns are Glowing (particularly since it's mid-February and pouring with rain!). O Dear and Lovely Brother, I Learned it in the Meadow Path followed by Hush My Dear Lie Still and Slumber. O for a Thousand Tongues to Sing – wishful thinking as only five people in the congregation opened their mouths – and of those I don't think Hark the Herald Angels Sing would have been too appropriate either!

'Seriously though, enough about print. I'm sure we're all agreed that Angela and Michael HAVE made the right choice in choosing each other.

'So, here's to Angela and Michael.

'Long may they keep open house to three of the best friends they'll ever have: Love, Life and Laughter!'

CHAPTER FOUR

Writing your Speech

Let us assume that you have read through the specimen speeches in Chapters Two and Three and that none of them seems quite what you are looking for, even when you've changed the names and facts to suit.

If time is short, you could try developing one of the specimen speeches. Using the basic format, you could take out the chunks that don't apply, or that you don't like, and add material of your own. Chapters Five and Six contain some quotations, toasts and jokes that may appeal to you. If, however, you change the content of a specimen speech, do keep a continuity, or flow, of sentences and style.

Otherwise, you are left with the option of writing your own speech, from 'scratch'. To many, this is a terrifying — or at best daunting — prospect. However, if you obey a few very elementary rules, and heed some guide-lines, you can succeed with comparative ease.

The first rule is: Always remember you are 'writing for speaking', not 'writing for reading'. This rule is vital if you are to produce a good speech. There is an unfortunate tendency among the inexperienced to come up with a piece of literature — rather like a school composition, or a report to the boss — instead of a speech. Indeed, it has to be said that many books of ready-made speeches on the library shelves are for 'reading', not for 'speaking'.

Although you won't want your style to seem slovenly, you needn't aim at the finer points of good grammar. In fact, if you do, you'll sound incredibly stilted. Use short sentences. If you don't, you'll very likely find yourself gasping for breath when you deliver your speech. Sentences beginning with 'And' or 'But' are fine, because we begin sentences in that way when we speak. Never use a long word if you are not 'easy' using it; you'll very likely stumble over it on the day! On the other hand, try to avoid slang and dialect words and phrases. You may think these 'relax' your style, but your audience may be 'uncomfortable' with them.

The second rule seems to be stating the obvious. This is: Speeches must have a beginning, a middle and an end. How many of you *know* you could produce a good speech, if only you could get started? So, *don't* 'get started'; begin in the middle!

You should, by now, have collected together as many facts and details about the wedding as you can. You should also know what those arranging the wedding would like you to cover, and what they would prefer you not to mention, in your speech.

List all the points you wish to make, and note any outstanding queries you may have. The lists for the three traditional speakers might look something like the following.

Bride's father

Welcome everybody/Thank helpers/Say how beautiful Kathy looks/Kathy's career/How proud we are/Welcome and praise Bob/Advice to them — perhaps quotation?/ Wish them happiness/Toast.

(Query: Call him Bob or Robert?/Check if any of Bob's close friends or relatives seriously ill.)

Bridegroom

Thank Beth and Jack for reception/Thank Jack for toast/ Thank him for welcome into family/Thank Mum and Dad for all they've done for me/Thank Stewart for being best man (Joke at his expense?)/Say how Kathy and I met and how lovely she looks/Praise the bridesmaids/Toast bridesmaids.

(Query: Check with Kathy that my joke is OK./Any feuds in Kathy's family to beware of?)

Best man

Thanks for toast to bridesmaids/Thanks for gifts to them/ Thanks that I'm best man (Joke)/Admire Kathy/Talk about Bob (Joke)/Wish them well (Quotation?)/Thank Beth and Jack on behalf of guests.

(Queries: Names of bridesmaids and how to pronounce them/Are they getting gifts?/Check if I'm to read telemessages/Is Kathy going to speak?/Check if there are any sensitive areas, in either family, to beware of/Check who will introduce the speakers.)

* * *

The next step is to make a draft of the middle and end sections of your speech. Cross off the items on your list as you include them in your draft. Remember, use short sentences, an easy style for speaking, and make your text flow. If you need help with the wording of a toast, the specimen speeches in Chapters Two and Three may help you, and there are other examples in Chapter Four.

When you feel your draft is reasonably to your liking, do a rough word count. Something of the order of 450 to 500 words for the middle and end sections will give you a speech of around 4 to 5 minutes. If it's much too long, edit out any repetitions and sentences that are not necessary, but still maintain your continuity. If it's still too long, it probably means you have a lot to say and, as long as it's not boring, a slightly over-long speech is no problem — you'll just be speaking for longer, that's all! If your draft is too short, why not add a suitable quotation or joke? But, do make it fit naturally into your text; it shouldn't sound as if it is padding for a short speech!

Now, it should be a fairly easy task to write in the start of your speech. You have tradition to fall back on if you can't find inspiration to be original. 'Ladies and Gentlemen' is the accepted opening, provided there are no guests of higher standing, in which case, for example,

'My Lord, Ladies and Gentlemen', or 'Reverend Green, Ladies and Gentlemen', should be the form used. Then, say something that will encourage your audience to listen.

If you are proposing the toast to the bride and groom, speak directly to the guests. Welcome them; perhaps mention some by name. If you are the bridegroom, your guests will expect you to say you are nervous and that you are a lucky chap. If you are the best man, you can thank the bride and groom — in a humorous fashion if you like — for choosing you as best man. If all else fails, the ideas for opening lines that follow are yours for the taking. Choose something that you feel comfortable with, and that will get you off to a flying start.

Some ideas for opening your speech

Ladies and Gentlemen — I'm nothing if not original!

Ladies and Gentlemen — You were expecting me to say that, weren't you?

Ladies and Gentlemen — Who says flattery doesn't work?

Ladies and Gentlemen — This is the happiest day of my life. What makes it so, is the lovely girl sitting next to me.

Ladies and Gentlemen — The bridegroom is expected to say that this is the happiest day of his life. So, tell me, all you husbands listening, does that mean my happiness is on the way downhill after today?

Ladies and Gentlemen — When you get older, three things start to happen. First, you lose your memory (pause and look blank) . . . I can't remember the other two things!

Friends — I'm not going to say very much, except that life is full of surprises, and my husband Peter is the best surprise that happened to me.

Friends — They tell me that marriage is a good thing. I've been thinking about that. Certainly, if it weren't for marriage, husbands and wives would have to argue with strangers!

Ladies and Gentlemen — They say that marriage is a lottery. If it is, then I must be the big winner.

Ladies and Gentlemen — I feel a little strange replying for the bridesmaids, because, as you can see, I'm not a bridesmaid!

Friends — I know you all too well to call you Ladies and Gentlemen.

Ladies and Gentlemen — Thank you for your kind introduction. I'll have to pray that you're forgiven for telling so many lies in praising me, and then pray for ME — for enjoying it so much!

Ladies and Gentlemen — I'm sure you know the three cardinal rules for after-dinner speakers: stand up, speak up, then shut up — well I shan't disappoint you, I'll do just that.

Ladies and Gentlemen — I'm sure you're all waiting for me to sing the groom's praises — only a couple of problems — I can't sing and I don't know the words anyway!

Ladies and Gentlemen — When I told my new father-in-law a few hours ago that I felt nervous about making this speech, he said: don't worry, everyone EXPECTS a groom to make a complete fool of himself, they'll be disappointed if you don't. And the last thing I want to do today is disappoint you!

* * *

When your draft speech is complete, keep it with you and look at it from time to time, perhaps polishing or improving it as you get new ideas. Have a word, if you can, with the other speechmakers at the wedding, so that you don't duplicate a joke or quotation and so that you know if some point will be raised to which you should reply or react. Do, however, keep the speech flowing!

CHAPTER FIVE

Useful Quotations and Toasts for your Speech

Quotations

An appropriate quotation, neatly led into, will add a touch of flavour to your speech. More than one quotation will probably sound pretentious in a fairly short speech.

Throw your quotation in lightly, develop on the theme, and, if you know its source, tell your audience. Here are some examples.

Example 1

'Ladies and Gentlemen — As I rise to propose the health of the bride and groom, I am reminded of the words of William Congreve. (Reminded, I should say by my wife, who looked the quotation up last night.)

'Congreve said: "Though marriage makes man and wife one flesh, it leaves 'em two fools." Now just take a look at our two young fools. They don't seem to mind their foolishness at all. On the contrary, they seem to be revelling in it.

'And when I look round at you distinguished people I can see quite a lot of old friends who have been two fools together for almost as long as have my wife and I.

'And they all seem perfectly happy in their foolishness. It is very pleasant, you know, to see through a thundering old cynic like Congreve. The most sensible thing a man can do is to find himself the right wife . . .'

Example 2

'. . . There used to be a popular song which had this refrain, if I remember it properly: "Love makes the world go round." Any schoolboy will tell you that the world goes round because it can't stop spinning on its axis. But looking at Diana and Chris today, I think it is perfectly true to say that it is love that makes *their* world go round . . .'

Example 3

'. . . You all know the old song: "Why am I always the bridesmaid, Never the blushing bride?" Well I feel like changing it a little and singing: "Why am I always the best man, Never the blushing bridegroom?" Because this is the third wedding at which I have been best man in eighteen months. If it goes on like this I shall lose my amateur status.

'Between you and me, I can tell you the real reason why I am on the shelf at twenty-five is that I've never met a girl like Anna . . .'

* * *

Quotations live on because they are, out of their original context, witty, pithy, apt, funny, cynical or even unkind. Never include an unkind quotation or toast in your speech. And do consider that what *you* find very funny, may be hurtful to someone listening to you. Cynical quotations may be used to good effect — as in Example 1, but, as in that example, the speaker should immediately distance the company present from such sentiments.

Here are some quotations that may appeal to you.

On Marriage

By all means marry. If you get a good wife you will become happy — and if you get a bad one you will become a philosopher.

Socrates

Any intelligent woman who reads the marriage contract, and then goes into it, deserves all the consequences.

Isadora Duncan

Marriage is a sort of friendship recognised by the police.

Marriage is a wonderful institution, but who wants to live in an institution?

Groucho Marx

It's a funny thing that when a man hasn't anything on earth to worry about, he goes off and gets married.

Robert Frost

Marriage is popular because it combines the maximum of temptation with the maximum of opportunity.

George Bernard Shaw

Marriage has many pains, but celibacy has no pleasures.

Samuel Johnson

God, the best maker of all marriages, combine your hearts in one.

William Shakespeare

What delight we married people have to see these poor fools decoyed into our condition.

Samuel Pepys

He's the most married man I ever saw.

Artemus Ward

Advice to persons about to marry — don't.

Punch, 1845

Marriages are made in heaven.

Alfred, Lord Tennyson

There are six requisites in every happy marriage. The first is Faith and the remaining five are Confidence.

Elbert Hubbard

Marriage is based on the theory that when a man

discovers a particular brand of beer exactly to his taste, he should at once throw up his job and go to work in the brewery.

George Jean Nathan

On Second Marriages

The triumph of hope over experience.
Dr Samuel Johnson

We are number two. We try harder.
Avis Car Rental Advertisement

When widows exclaim loudly against second marriages, I would always lay a wager that the man, if not the wedding day, is absolutely fixed on.

Henry Fielding

For I'm not so old, and not so plain. And I'm quite prepared to marry again.
W. S. Gilbert

Socrates died from an overdose of wedlock.
Answer to an Examination Question

I chose my wife, as she did her wedding gown, for qualities that would wear well.
Oliver Goldsmith

On Husbands and Wives

Being a husband is a whole time job.
Arnold Bennett

All husbands are alike, but they have different faces so you can tell them apart.

A husband is a man who, two minutes after his head touches the pillow, is snoring like an overloaded omnibus.

Ogden Nash

It is true that all married men have their own way, but the trouble is they don't all have their own way of having it!

Artemus Ward

A husband's last words are always, 'OK, buy it!'

Being a husband is just like any other job; it's much easier if you like your boss.

A model husband is one, who when his wife is away, washes the dishes every day. Both of them!

If a husband has troubles, he should tell his wife. If he hasn't, he should tell the world how he does it.

Nothing makes a good wife like a good husband.

The world well tried — the sweetest thing in life, is the unclouded welcome of a wife.

N. P. Willis

Husbands, love your wives, and be not bitter against them.

The Bible

Whoso findeth a wife, findeth a good thing.

The Bible

Who follows his wife in everything is an ignoramus.

The Talmud

An ideal wife is any woman who has an ideal husband.

Booth Tarkington

When a woman gets married, it's like jumping into a hole in the ice in the middle of winter. You do it once and you remember it the rest of your days.

Maxim Gorky

Every man who is high up likes to feel that he has done it all himself. And the wife smiles and lets it go at that. It's our only joke. Every woman knows that.

J. M. Barrie

The man who says his wife can't take a joke, forgets that she took him.

No man should have a secret from his wife. She invariably finds it out.

Oscar Wilde

Various

Never argue at the dinner table, for the one who is not hungry always gets the best of the argument.

Richard Whately

Ninety per cent of the friction in daily life is caused by the tone of voice.

Arnold Bennett

Whatever women do, they must do twice as well as men to be thought half as good. Luckily, this is not difficult.

Charlotte Whitton

Love is more than gold or great riches.

John Lydgate

Love and marriage go together like a horse and carriage.

Song — Sammy Cahn

Love carries all before him. We too must yield to Love.

Virgil

There's no place like home, after the other places close.

Be sure to leave other men their turns to speak.

Francis Bacon

The great question which I have never been able to answer is, 'What does a woman want?'

Sigmund Freud

Women like silent men. They think they're listening.

Marcel Achard

A wise man makes more opportunities than he finds.

Francis Bacon

There are two times in a man's life when he should not speculate: when he can't afford it, and when he can.

Mark Twain

The most dangerous food a man can eat is wedding cake.

American Proverb

There is nothing in the world like the devotion of a married woman. It's a thing no married man knows anything about.

Oscar Wilde

The only premarital thing girls don't do these days is cooking.

Omar Sharif

I often quote myself; it adds spice to my conversation.

George Bernard Shaw

An optimist is a fellow who believes a housefly is looking for a way to get out.

George Jean Nathan

Money won't buy happiness, but it will pay the salaries of a large research staff to study the problem.

Bill Vaughan

When a man sits with a pretty girl for an hour, it seems like a minute. But let him sit on a hot stove for a minute — and it's longer than any hour. That's relativity.

Albert Einstein

Many a man in love with a dimple, makes the mistake of marrying the whole girl.

Stephen Leacock

'My father gave me these hints on speechmaking: be sincere, be brief, be seated.'

James Roosevelt

'If you don't strike oil in ten minutes, stop boring.'

To Conclude the Quotations

'I WOULD pretend that these quotations came straight from memory, that's if Michael hadn't caught me with a book of quotations last week.'

'I must confess, I'd never heard that quotation until yesterday when someone suggested it to me and it seemed so apt to pass it on to you today — though you probably all knew it anyway.'

Some Less Traditional Toasts

Some speechmakers like to get away from the age-old toasts for good luck, health, happiness and may all your troubles be little ones. Here are a few examples of toasts which are less traditional. They could be particularly useful at small, informal wedding receptions where you don't want to sound pompous.

'To our friends: May Fortune be as generous with them as she has been in giving us such friends.'

'To husbands: Men when they are boys; boys when they are men; and lovable always.'

'Long life and happiness — for your long life will be my happiness.'

'To the bride and groom: May we all be invited to your Golden Wedding celebrations.'

'To the bride: May she share everything with her husband, including the housework.'

To the bridegroom: He is leaving us for a better life. But we are not leaving him.'

'May you live as long as you like, and have all you like as long as you live.'

'To the lamp of true friendship. May it burn brightest in our darkest hours and never flicker in the winds of trial.'

'As Sydney Smith wrote: Here's to marriage. That happy estate that resembles a pair of scissors, so joined that they cannot be separated, often moving in opposite directions, yet punishing anyone that comes between them.'

'Live today to the fullest! Remember, it's the first day of the rest of your life.'

'To that nervous, fidgety, restless, impatient, uncomfortable but enviable fellow, the groom.'

'To the bride: Let her remember that we give her this husband on approval. He can be returned for credit or exchange, but her love will not be refunded.'

'Here's to your happy launching of the *Courtship* on the Sea of Matrimony. May the rocks be confined to the cradle!'

'To the happy bridesmaids: Who today proved the truth of Tennyson's sonnet — "A happy bridesmaid makes a happy bride." '

'To the bride and groom: May the roof above you never fall in and may you both never fall out.'

'To the bride and groom: As you slide down the banister of life, may the splinters never face the wrong way!'

'To the bride and groom: I wish you health, I wish you happiness, I wish you wealth, I wish you heaven — what more could I wish?'

CHAPTER SIX

Some Jokes and Humorous Anecdotes

A suitable joke or humorous anecdote can do much to lighten a speech which would, otherwise, be all 'praise and thanks'. More than one — or two at the most — will make a fairly short speech seem like a comic routine. And, as we all know, some comedians' acts can go very flat indeed! You don't want the guests rolling in the aisles, and you don't want them grim with embarrassment or muttering, 'I really didn't understand that one!'.

If you can adapt a joke to suit the situation, so much the better. But never include in your speech any joke or story that could possibly hurt or offend anyone present. Aim at raising a smile, not at raising a belly laugh. And do remember, it's the way you tell 'em, that makes them successful. Lead into your joke naturally and keep it short — so neither you nor your audience loses track of it halfway through.

Here is a selection that you may find useful. Some, but not all, are about weddings and brides and grooms.

For the Bride's Father

Les says he's a keen football fan and that he's an Arsenal supporter. I don't quite see the connection!

* * *

When Tessa was a small girl, she came home crying that a big girl had hit her. Her mother said, 'Which big girl? Did you hit her back?' 'Oh no,' said Tessa. 'I hit her first!'

* * *

Things have changed. When we came home from work, we used to say, 'What's cooking?' Nowadays, it's 'What's thawing?'

* * *

Two men were sitting on the bank of a river, fishing. It was Sunday morning and the church bells were pealing in the nearby village. 'I feel a bit guilty,' said one. 'We shouldn't be here, we should have gone to church.' 'I don't feel guilty at all,' said the other. 'I couldn't have gone to church anyway. My wife's sick in bed.'

* * *

The best way to remember your wife's birthday is to forget it once.

* * *

Some people make the mistake of marrying for better or worse but not for good.

* * *

We men never quite understand the phrase 'professional women'. . . . Are there any amateurs?

* * *

The bride sobbed to her husband, 'Oh dear, I was pressing your suit and the iron burnt a hole in the trousers!' Husband comforted her. 'Now, don't you worry. That suit has two pairs of trousers.' 'Yes, I know,' said the wife, 'I used the second pair to patch the hole!'

* * *

Adam: 'Eve, do you really love me?'
Eve: 'Who else?'

* * *

Someone once said that marriage is what teaches a man frugality, regularity, temperance — and other virtues he wouldn't have needed if he'd stayed single.

* * *

After the honeymoon, husband says to wife, 'You wouldn't mind if I pointed out a few of your little defects, would you?' 'Not at all dear,' she replied sweetly. 'It was those little defects that stopped me from getting a better husband.'

An estate agent was showing a woman around a large house. 'I could do a lot with this,' she said. Then added, 'On the other hand, I think that was what I said the first time I saw my husband.'

For the Bridegroom

Brian is a really tolerant person. He always says, 'Be tolerant with those people who disagree with you. They have a right to their ridiculous opinions.'

* * *

The first time I dated Shirley, her father said she was just putting the finishing touches to her make-up, but she'd be down in a minute. Then he added, 'Care for a game of chess?'

* * *

I've been told that a glass of champagne will cure all sorts of ills. All you need is a candle. You light the candle, drink the glass and wait five minutes. Then, drink another glass, still watching the candle. You keep this up until you can see three candles. Then, you blow out the middle one, and go to sleep.

* * *

Bob is a statistician. One day a young chap came up to him and said, 'Spare 10p mate, I haven't eaten for a week!' Bob got out his notebook. 'Really,' he replied. 'And how does that compare with the same period last year?'

My best man's trimmed his dangling locks, he's cut and
let them fall.
And all because of what he called, 'The cruellest words of
all.'
So now he's past the long-hair stage. And though I'm no
contriver,
It did me good to hear him called, 'A crazy woman
driver.'

*   *   *

Today, I've been given two very useful pieces of advice.
The first is: Try praising your wife — even if it does
frighten her at first. The second: If you don't at first
succeed, do it the way your wife told you.

*   *   *

The brain is a wonderful thing. It never stops working
from the time you are born until the moment you start to
make a speech.

*   *   *

She: 'Can we get married soon?'
He: 'But, we won't be able to afford a home for years!
She: 'We could live with your Mum and Dad!'
He: 'That just isn't possible. They're still living with
      Dad's Mum and Dad.'

*   *   *

It's funny how many women like a man with a past. Of
course, a man with a present is still very popular.

And so to my best man, Charlie. People have asked me about Charlie's job. I say he's a visual display technician. That's because he asked me not to tell anyone that he's a window cleaner.

* * *

Patrick, my best man, is a stout fellow. Well, stout, beer, ale, champagne. . .

For the Best Man

Two middle-aged ladies were talking about marriage. 'I haven't seen my husband for twenty years,' said one. 'He went out to buy a cabbage, and never came back.' 'What on earth did you do?' asked the other. 'Oh, I just opened a tin of peas.'

* * *

Here is a wedding day weather forecast. Two warm fronts are converging, followed later by a little sun.

* * *

'Sorry, we've sold right out of geraniums in pots,' said the girl at the garden centre. 'What about some nice pots of chrysanths?' 'Oh, no,' said the customer. 'It was geraniums my wife told me to water while she was away.'

* * *

Many couples are unhappily married, but unfortunately they don't know it.

*   *   *

Husband: 'In our six years of marriage, we haven't been able to agree on a single thing!'
Wife: 'No, it's been seven years, dear!'

*   *   *

Gerry said he knew Debra could keep a secret. They'd been engaged for weeks before he knew anything about it!

*   *   *

Lisa and Ken are very independent people. I don't think they are as independent as one married couple I heard of, though. *They* sent individual Christmas cards! To the same people!

*   *   *

Jack, remember there's no place like home! Well, after the other places close, anyway!

*   *   *

Somebody once said, 'No speech can be really bad, if it's short enough.' Mine will be short! Some of the best people hated making speeches. Orville and Wilbur Wright, for example. Once, at an important function, Wilbur was called upon by the toastmaster. 'There must be a mistake,' stammered Wilbur. 'Orville is the one who does the speaking.' The toastmaster turned to Orville. He rose and announced, 'Wilbur just made the speech.'

*　*　*

Always remember, Jane and Roger, misfortune is a point of view. No doubt, your headaches feel good to an aspirin salesman!

*　*　*

There was this fellow who discovered a way to hammer in nails without hitting his thumb. He got his wife to hold the nail.

For a Small Wedding Reception

At small and informal wedding receptions, the speeches will generally be very short — in fact, little more than toasts. After the cake has been cut, the guests will probably circulate and chatter amongst themselves.

When this happens, there is always the risk of the happy atmosphere turning a little miserable; the conversation turning to hospitals and operations at one end of the room and to TV, sex and heavy drinking skills at the other. The bride may well be hissing, 'Somebody, do break up the cliques. Everybody should mix and be happy! Doesn't anyone know a funny story?' Here are a few, general, funny stories that might help to brighten things up and give the guests a chance to swap groups and circulate.

A mother and small daughter go into a police station. 'I want to report a missing person,' said the mother. 'Certainly madam,' replied the desk sergeant, 'can you give me a brief description?' 'Well, he's over six foot tall, blond, blue eyed and about twenty-eight years old.' 'But Mummy, that doesn't sound anything like Daddy,' the small girl interrupted. 'You be quiet!' said her mother. 'We don't want *him* back.'

* * *

The vicar's wife called round to welcome the newlyweds who had just moved into their new home in the village. As she rang the doorbell a large dog came up to her, wagging its tail happily. She was invited in and the dog accompanied her, settling itself alongside her on the brand new settee. After a chat and a cup of tea, she rose to leave — but to her horror, the dog jumped down, walked over to the standard lamp and solemnly lifted one leg. There was an extremely large puddle. Then the dog squatted. A large pile was added. The newlyweds smiled sweetly and completely ignored the dog's activities. The vicar's wife left rather hurriedly, and as she reached the garden gate she heard her name called. 'Excuse us, but you've forgotten your dog!' called the newlyweds.

* * *

A customs officer, an MP, a vicar and a boy scout were aboard an aircraft which went out of control. The pilot ejected and there were only three parachutes to be found. The customs officer took one. 'I'm needed in the fight against smuggling,' he cried as he jumped. The member of parliament took the second. 'My constituents need me,' was his cry as he, too, leaped from the plane. The vicar smiled at the young boy. 'I have lived a good Christian life and I shall go to heaven immediately. You take the last parachute.' 'That's very good of you, sir,' answered the boy scout. 'But we have a parachute each. That customs officer took my rucksack'.

*   *   *

The firm's boss was under stress. The business was not doing at all well. His doctor recommended a week's rest at a small nursing home in the country. After a few days he was much improved. However, the following week the firm was phoned and told that, sadly he had suffered a relapse. 'What happened?' asked the deputy boss. 'Well,' said the nursing sister, 'he said he was a bit bored, so we suggested he could help by sorting out the whites from the coloureds in the laundry room.' 'Oh my goodness!' cried the deputy boss, 'you don't mean you asked him to make *decisions?*'

*   *   *

Tommy was late returning home from a friend's party and his parents were very worried. The phone rang. 'This is me, Tommy, the train broke down and we were put on a bus and I'm in a phone box and I don't know where I am!' 'I'll come and pick you up,' said Dad. 'On the wall under the mirror you'll see a card and on it will be the address of the phone box.' There was a very long pause. Then, 'Dad, I can't get the mirror off the wall!'

*   *   *

'How old are you, Granny?' the small girl asked. 'I don't remember, dear,' said the grandmother. 'You could look in your knickers,' said the child, helpfully. 'Mine say how old I am. Look! Four to five years old!'

* * *

The group sat around the table, their fingers touching. 'Is there anybody there?' asked the medium. After a while, a cheery voice echoed round the room. 'Hi, Mary, this is me, George.' 'Goodness me,' cried one of the group. 'It's my late husband. How are you, dear? What's it like where you are?' 'Not too bad,' George's voice came back. 'The food's a bit boring though. Nothing but salads and more salads.' 'But do you feel loved, George?' asked Mary. 'Loved!' replied George. 'I don't know about loved, but there's more sex on offer than I can manage.' 'Oh dear, George,' cried Mary. 'Do you think you are in heaven or the other place?' 'Neither,' said George confidently. 'I'm a (expletive) rabbit!'

* * *

Two cannibals came across a beautiful maiden, walking in the jungle. 'Uncle Reg,' said the younger cannibal. 'Look at that beautiful maiden, let's take her home with us and put her in the cooking pot!' 'I've got a much better idea,' replied Uncle Reg, licking his lips. So they took her home and put Aunt Mabel in the cooking pot.

* * *

Bert was responsible for security on a huge building site. Fred was a happy-go-lucky labourer on the site. Bert always knew that Fred was helping himself to things that were not his, but he could never catch him. Every night Fred would push his barrow through the gate and every night Bert would stop him and make a thorough search. This went on for weeks, but Bert never found a stolen item. Many, many years after, the two met up by chance in a pub. 'Fred,' said Bert, 'I've retired now, but I've always wondered what you were up to on that building site. I know you were stealing something, but what?' Fred took a long swig from his glass. 'Wheelbarrows!' he said, triumphantly.

* * *

Stan was in court. 'You are the defendant, and you plead not guilty to stealing Farmer Brown's chickens, is that correct?' asked the magistrate. 'I plead not guilty,' answered Stan, 'but I'm not the defendant. I'm only the chap who stole the chickens.'

* * *

Lucy, when a very small girl, was sitting on her mother's knee looking through a picture book of Bible stories. Before long they came to a drawing showing Christians being fed to the lions. Lucy started to cry and her mother tried to calm her by telling her that the Christians would soon be with Jesus. Lucy still wept. 'It's not fair,' she sobbed, 'that baby lion in the corner hasn't got a Christian!'

* * *

A woman who was delighted with the effect some beauty treatment was having on her, wrote to tell the beautician: 'Since my course of treatment, I'm a different woman. My husband is delighted!'

*   *   *

They had been married a year when the wife confessed that she'd splashed out his money on ten new pairs of shoes. 'Ten!' he exploded, 'What could you possibly want with ten new pairs of shoes?' She smiled at him fondly, 'Ten new handbags' she explained.

*   *   *

I heard someone in the wedding party complaining about the suit he'd bought for the wedding and saying that most sensible people hired theirs. I said 'Think yourself lucky, they've lowered mine!'

*   *   *

Did you see that drunk walking down the street with one shoe on? A policeman said to him 'Did you lose a shoe?' The drunk said 'No. I found one!'

*   *   *

When your daughter gets married and leaves home, people say, to cheer you up, 'You're not losing a daughter, you're gaining a son.' I'm luckier than that, I'm also gaining a telephone!

*   *   *

I'm sure that we all know that women should have genuine equality these days and I'm the first one to agree that this is only fair. I only said so to my wife this morning as she was cleaning my car. Isn't that right Jean?

83

"THE BRAIN IS A WONDERFUL THING. IT NEVER STOPS WORKING FROM THE TIME YOU ARE BORN UNTIL THE MOMENT YOU START TO MAKE A SPEECH."
NOTES

CHAPTER SEVEN

Rehearsing your Speech

Having written your speech you are about halfway to becoming a successful speechmaker. You still have some work to do on your presentation. Parallel your situation, if you like, with that of an actor. An actor may know his lines perfectly, but he needs direction, rehearsal and self-discipline to make a success of the part he is to play.

How will you know your lines?

You could read from your script. This is certainly the easiest way for you to present your speech, but it's not good from the viewpoint of the guests at the wedding. They will expect to be spoken to, not read to.

You could do as an actor does; that is, learn your speech by heart and then recite it. But, are you a good enough actor to sound 'natural'? Are you sure you won't forget your lines? And, if you have to make any last minute changes to your speech, will you get confused?

Most speechmakers find that the best way of presenting a fairly short speech is to compromise between reading it and reciting it. This involves getting thoroughly familiar with the content, but learning by heart only the vital facts, such as names, and how to pronounce them.

* * *

The content of your speech is not just the words, it is also its shape and structure. On your 'script', use a coloured felt pen to mark all the paragraph starts — the places where your theme changes. Use a different colour to mark in 'pauses'. Here, you will pause for effect or for an expected laugh or other reaction from your audience.

Pause markings are invaluable in your speech presentation. You will be able to see a little ahead, just where you can, for instance, clear your throat, or take a sip of water, without breaking the flow of your words.

* * *

Now, read through your speech several times, first in your head, then out loud. After a while, you will find you are so familiar with the speech that you can look up from your script from time to time, and then refer to it again to bring you back on course.

Before long, you will need to refer to your script only occasionally. You will be sufficiently familiar with it.

Performance

By now, you should have a clear idea of the size of your audience and the size of the room in which the reception will be held. With a small number of guests in a small room, you'll be able to be heard speaking in your normal voice — unless you normally speak very quietly. If it is to be a large hall, with many guests, microphones may well be provided, so again, your normal voice will be fine. If there are no microphones, you will need to work on your voice volume, so that you reach those at the back, but without shouting.

* * *

Try a non-dress rehearsal, one day when you are alone. Stand behind a table with a chair behind you. Have a tumbler of water and a glass of wine in front of you. Prop a large mirror at the far side of the table. This will represent your audience, and will also show you what they will see.

Perform your speech. Speak more slowly than you do normally, but not *too* slowly. Remember, the guests will be seated and you will be standing, so look out, as if over them with your head inclined slightly downwards. Smile, now and then, as you speak and let your gaze wander over all the guests. When you are referring to a particular person, turn your body — without shuffling your feet — so that you will be looking in the direction of that person. When you get to the toast, pick up your glass and drink the toast.

Now, be really critical of your performance, and see where it can be improved.

Did you wobble about — or, even worse, sway to and fro? Most inexperienced speechmakers do! Adjust the position of your feet, so that they are firmly planted and a little apart so that you feel relaxed and comfortable.

Were you able to hold your script easily? A piece of cardboard at the back would stop it flapping about. Or, you might prefer to write it out on a series of cards that you can hold in the palm of your hand. If you choose this method, make sure each card ends at the end of a paragraph and do number the cards clearly, so that they cannot get out of order. A loose tag through the cards would make sure they stayed in order and that one was not dropped at a crucial time.

Did you wave your free arm about? An occasional gesture is fine; it prevents you from appearing 'wooden'. But too much arm waving is wrong.

Delivery

You should, by now, know your speech quite well and you'll be aware of how you will look to your audience. You've got your voice level right for the room you'll be speaking in, so now you should check that your rate of speaking and your voice quality are satisfactory.

* * *

Practise your speech with the aid of the microphone supplied with most tape recorders and cassette players, setting the microphone well away from you if your voice will have to carry, without amplification, to the back of a large hall. Listen to your recorded speech and, again, be critical of yourself.

*   *   *

Perhaps you need to speak more slowly or more distinctly? Perhaps you should try to lower the pitch of your voice a little? Are you breathing properly? Take in a good breath at the beginning of each sentence and let it out easily as you speak. Never empty your lungs completely before taking another breath.

Are you concerned that you have an accent — local or foreign? Don't be! And don't try to 'talk posh' when it's not natural to you. However, don't be sloppy about pronunciation — especially of people's names, and do take a little care over your h's and over words ending in 'd', 't' and '-ing'. You will then, not only sound more professional, but you'll be understood.

Best man — introduction of speakers

If you are the best man you will know if there is to be a professional toastmaster at the reception or if it will fall to you to introduce those making the speeches. If the task falls to you, now is the time for you to try out your statements of introduction.

*   *   *

Yours will be the first voice the guests hear as they sit, replete, awaiting the speeches. You must command attention and your few words must be understood. Practise standing up straight, smiling pleasantly, and saying very clearly: 'Ladies and Gentlemen — The father of the bride'; or: 'Ladies and Gentlemen — Mr John Brown will now propose a toast to the bride and groom', where the bride's father is not proposing the toast.

Your second introduction can be equally simple. 'Ladies and Gentlemen — the groom' or 'Ladies and Gentlemen — the groom will now reply to the toast' will be sufficient.

How you introduce yourself will need to be discussed with the bridegroom. He may wish to introduce you at the end of his speech, especially if he has proposed the toast to the bridesmaids early in his speech or if there are no bridesmaids. He will end by saying something like: 'And now it's the turn of Sam, my best man, to say a few words to you.' If you have to introduce yourself, all you need say is: 'Ladies and Gentlemen — I expect you've realised by now that I am the best man,' and then give your own speech.

If the bride wishes to speak, introduce her after you have read any telemessages with something very encouraging, like: "I'm sure you'll be delighted that the bride is now going to say a few words to us all. Ladies and Gentlemen — the bride.'

* * *

So, along with practising the performance and delivery of your speech, do give some attention to the performance and delivery of your introductions. It is a simple task, but it needs doing well.

Dress rehearsal

About a week before the wedding, arrange a dress rehearsal. Put on a good suit and set out the table, chair and glasses as before. If you have, or can borrow, a flash camera and a video camera, these will be very useful, since at many modern weddings, the speeches are punctuated with the flashes from amateur camerapersons and the panning and zooming of video buffs.

*   *   *

Invite your wife, or a friend whose opinion you trust, to be your audience of one. Tell them that your speech is in its final state and that, unless you have made any dreadful errors, it will not be changed. Ask them to video you as you deliver your speech and to occasionally take a flash photograph — or at least make the camera flash, occasionally.

*   *   *

Reassure them that you are not seeking a professional film of your dress rehearsal, but just atmosphere. What you do need is a valued opinion on your performance of the speech. Above all, can you be heard and understood, but also, have you any irritating habits that you are unaware of, but which might annoy the wedding guests? We all have such involuntary habits as needlessly pushing up spectacles, rubbing the nose, or brushing back the hair. You must do your utmost to keep these under strict control for the time of your speech.

*   *   *

Hopefully, your valued audience of one will applaud your speech, or at least say, 'Well, I've heard a lot worse!' And, of course, you can always view the video film he or she took, to confirm the opinion.

* * *

Now, you will have reaped the benefit of your efforts. You will feel more self-confident. You will feel sure that you have prepared a good speech and that you will present it competently.

CHAPTER EIGHT

Stand and Deliver!

There are three important things to remember on the big day. The first is vital! Before you leave for the wedding, and again at the reception, check that you have the script of your speech with you. The second is more advisory. Don't imbibe too much prior to making your speech. You may think an extra glass of wine will relax you, but the chances are that it will, instead, make you woolly-headed. The third is for your own comfort and well-being. Even if you don't feel the need, visit the toilet about ten minutes before the speeches are due to start.

The Preliminaries ...

If there is a toastmaster, he will make sure the guests' glasses are filled, the microphones — if such there are — are well placed and working, and the speechmakers are in place and ready. He will then call for the guests' attention and announce the first speechmaker.

Where there are no microphones, it is a good idea if those organising the wedding ask a reliable guest — perhaps an usher — to stand at the back of the room to signal to the speakers that their voices are reaching all. This will avoid the unprofessional 'Can you hear me at the back?' 'No!' routine, which can be distracting to guests and speaker alike.

* * *

Those guests with video cameras should have been asked to stay in their seats during the speeches — so as not to distract the speechmakers or obstruct the guests' view.

Just in case there are badly behaved children or noisy elements among the guests, it would be advisable to ask a few friends to stand by so that they can deal gently and politely with potential problem areas early on.

* * *

When there is no toastmaster, the job of gaining the attention of the guests and announcing the speakers normally falls to the best man. If you are the best man, you will know what is expected of you and will be poised to introduce the opening speaker at the appropriate time.

The guests, having had their glasses filled, will be anticipating the speeches, so a light tap on a tumbler, and a call for attention — with a friendly smile — should do the trick. Then, making sure that the opening speechmaker is ready for action, you can make the introduction.

... and 'Action!'

Now to you, the speechmaker. Before you rise to make your speech, check where anyone to whom you'll be referring is seated — so that you can look in their direction at the appropriate moment. Know where your handkerchief is — in case you need it — and make sure your water tumbler and wine glass are to hand, but not in danger of being knocked over.

*   *   *

When your big moment arrives, tell yourself how calm and well-prepared you are. Stand, and pause for an instant, remembering to smile as you gaze over the guests. They will smile back, encouragingly, and you can begin to address them.

Remember, you are not racing against the clock. If a joke in your speech causes a laugh or a murmur, be happy that your audience is 'with you', and wait, smiling, for quiet before proceeding.

For the time that you are delivering your speech, you are in charge. If you should be so unfortunate as to be faced with an ill-mannered guest who interrupts you, wait for him to be silent — or to be politely silenced by others — and then carry on without comment. Should you find you've made a mistake, smile and say 'Sorry!' — but without becoming flustered. Then correct your error.

*   *   *

Then, it will be all over and you'll be sitting down to the

smiles of appreciation and the applause. Was it worth all the preparation? Of course it was! You were a successful speechmaker! Congratulations!